T0109690

The cost of liberty is less than the price of repression.

— W.E.B. DU BOIS
JOHN BROWN: A BIOGRAPHY, 1909

By the President of the United States of Ame

A Proclamation.

Whereas, on the twenty-second day
September, in the year of our Lord one thous
eight hundred and sixty-two, a proclamate
was issued by the President of the United Sta
containing, among other things, the followi
to wit:

"That on the first day of January, in
"year of our Lord one thousand eight hundr
"and sixty-three, all persons held as slaves u
"any State or designated part of a State, the pe
"whereof shall then be in rebellion against th
"United States, shall be then, thenceforward, a
"forever free; and the Executive Government of
"United States, including the military and na
"authority thereof, will recognize and mainta
"the freedom of such persons, and will do no
"or acts to repress such persons, or any of the
"in any efforts they may make for their actua
"freedom.

"That the Executive will, on the first.

THE
EMANCIPATION
PROCLAMATION

And Other Documents of Freedom

SMITHSONIAN EDITION

SMITHSONIAN BOOKS · WASHINGTON, DC

Published by Smithsonian Books
Director: Carolyn Gleason
Editor: Julie Huggins

Edited by Joanne Reams
Designed by Robert L. Wiser

This book may be purchased for educational, business, or sales promotional use. For information, please write:

Special Markets Department, Smithsonian Books, P.O. Box 37012, MRC 513, Washington, DC 20013

Library of Congress Cataloging-in-Publication Data available upon request.

ISBN 978-1-58834-708-4

Printed in the United States of America

26   25   24   23   22   2   3   4   5

Transcriptions and images from the National Archives, except Law Enacting Emancipation in the Federal Territories transcription from the Freedmen and Southern Society Project, University of Maryland; photograph on page 6 courtesy of the National Museum of American History; and photographs on pages 9, 11, and 32 courtesy of the National Museum of African American History and Culture.

Contents

In 1862, President Abraham Lincoln sat at a desk in
the War Department telegraph office and, using
this inkstand, drafted a presidential order to free the
enslaved people held in Confederate states.

Introduction

ON SEPTEMBER 22, 1862, Abraham Lincoln issued the preliminary Emancipation Proclamation. Under his wartime authority as commander-in-chief, he ordered that as of January 1, 1863, enslaved individuals in all areas still in rebellion against the United States "henceforward shall be free." On New Years' Day, the day the Emancipation Proclamation was signed, cannon shots fired, church bells rang, and speakers orated at public observances throughout the North and in Union-held areas of the South. January 1, formerly known among the enslaved as "Heartbreak Day" for the large slave auctions often held, would be known henceforth as a day of deliverance and jubilee.

In Union-held Beaufort, South Carolina, Colonel Thomas Wentworth Higginson presided over a ceremony where the Proclamation was read publicly. After the reading, Higginson related, he waved the flag and there arose from among the freed slaves on hand an "elderly male voice, into which two women's voices instantly blended, singing . . . 'My Country, 'tis of thee, Sweet land of liberty.'. . . I never saw anything so electric; it made all other words cheap . . . the life of the whole day was in those unknown people's song."

The Proclamation was carried and read as portions of the South were occupied. Every advance of the Union army thus became a liberating step, providing for the nation the possibility of what Abraham Lincoln in his Gettysburg address called "a new birth of freedom." As Frederick Douglass, one of the individuals who had the greatest influence on Lincoln in issuing the document declared, "We are all liberated by this Proclamation. . . . The white man is liberated, the black man is liberated."

Even though the Emancipation Proclamation was made effective in 1863, it could not be implemented in places still under Confederate control. As a result, in the westernmost Confederate state of Texas, nominal freedom came on June 19, 1865, when some two thousand Union troops arrived in Galveston Bay, Texas, at the end of the Civil War, and announced that enslaved Black people in the state were no longer in bondage, although most held in slavery had not waited to be freed. This day came to be known as "Juneteenth" by African Americans in Texas, heralding our country's second Independence Day and now officially recognized as a national holiday. By the end of the war, millions of enslaved people, some with the assistance of the US Army and the federal government, had seized their own freedom.

The story of the Emancipation Proclamation, one of the most important documents of freedom in American history, and the wider story of emancipation of which it is a vital part, was never inevitable. The process through which the Proclamation was crafted reveals a deeper and wider story about the meaning of freedom in America and the paradox of liberty in a nation founded with slavery structured into the Constitution and a mainspring of its economic, social, and political life. It also provides a window into a long story of freedom seeking and making by African Americans that continues to have deep meaning today.

President Lincoln drafted the Emancipation Proclamation as a matter of military and diplomatic necessity

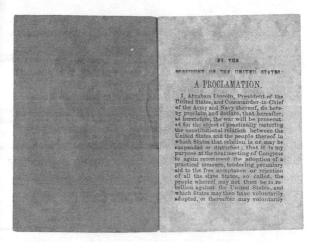

This booklet was produced in December 1862 for Union soldiers to read and distribute among African Americans.

but also because of his growing recognition of abolition as a matter of moral necessity and his ongoing struggle to embrace wider rights of African Americans within the nation—all of which continued up until his assassination. He hoped to undermine the Confederate war effort by declaring enslaved people free in only those ten rebellious states. Nonetheless, emancipation became a moral and social imperative. Long before the Proclamation was envisioned, Black abolitionists along with white allies had fostered a decades-long movement and political crisis that seized upon wartime conditions and led in 1862 to the emancipation acts in federal territories and the nation's capital, Washington, DC. Enslaved African Americans who had sought freedom for generations further forced collective emancipation by fleeing to Union camps by the tens of thousands.

In the nation's capital Lincoln himself witnessed African American freedom claims as he passed through tent cities built by fugitives from slavery.

While the Proclamation was limited and conservative by intent, its impact was revolutionary. The Civil War, which began as a war to preserve the Union, was transformed by the stroke of a pen into a war to end slavery, yoking the project of freedom for all to the very survival of the nation. Its repercussions meant more than just the end of slavery. It signaled the possibility of a second founding for America—one that included the potential for African Americans to find equality as full citizens in American society.

The Thirteenth Amendment, issued on December 6, 1865, completed what free and enslaved African Americans, abolitionists, and the Emancipation Proclamation had set in motion, formally abolishing slavery throughout the United States. The Fourteenth and Fifteenth Amendments provided equal protection of the law for all citizens, extended the vote to Black men, and banned racial discrimination in voting. They transformed the United States into the first interracial democracy in world history, albeit one that continued to be threatened by segregation, injustice, and racial violence.

The struggle to fulfill the promises of liberty, equality, and justice for all would continue for generations to come. In this struggle for fuller freedom, we find the roots of many movements for civil and human rights that exist today, demonstrating that the work of seeking equality and justice for all in the United States is unfinished and ongoing.

— PAUL GARDULLO

The Fifteenth Amendment gave all male citizens the right to vote regardless of race or previous condition of servitude. This central scene from a lithograph honoring the amendment depicts a Baltimore parade held on May 19, 1870, that drew a celebratory crowd of more than twenty thousand. Above the parade are pictured influential Black abolitionists Martin R. Delany, Frederick Douglass, and Hiram Revels.

THE
EMANCIPATION
PROCLAMATION

By the PRESIDENT of the UNITED STATES OF AMERICA:

A PROCLAMATION.

———

Whereas, on the twenty-second day of September, in the year of our Lord one thousand eight hundred and sixty-two, a proclamation was issued by the President of the United States, containing, among other things, the following, to wit:

"That on the first day of January, in the year of our Lord one thousand eight hundred and sixty-three, all persons held as slaves within any State or designated part of a State, the people whereof shall then be in rebellion against the United States, shall be then, thenceforward, and forever free; and the Executive Government of the United States, including the military and naval authority thereof, will recognize and maintain the freedom of such persons, and will do no act or acts to repress such persons, or any of them, in any efforts they may make for their actual freedom.

"That the Executive will, on the first day of January aforesaid, by proclamation, designate the States and parts of States, if any, in which the people thereof, respectively, shall then be in rebellion against the United States; and the fact that any State, or the people thereof, shall on that day be, in good faith, represented in the Congress of the United States by members chosen thereto at elections wherein a majority of the qualified voters of such State shall have participated, shall, in the absence of strong countervailing testimony, be deemed conclusive evidence that such

State, and the people thereof, are not then in rebellion against the United States."

———

Now, therefore I, ABRAHAM LINCOLN, PRESIDENT OF THE UNITED STATES, by virtue of the power in me vested as Commander-in-Chief, of the Army and Navy of the United States in time of actual armed rebellion against the authority and government of the United States, and as a fit and necessary war measure for suppressing said rebellion, do, on this first day of January, in the year of our Lord one thousand eight hundred and sixty-three, and in accordance with my purpose so to do publicly proclaimed for the full period of one hundred days, from the day first above mentioned, order and designate as the States and parts of States wherein the people thereof respectively, are this day in rebellion against the United States, the following, to wit: ARKANSAS, TEXAS, LOUISIANA, (except the Parishes of St. Bernard, Plaquemines, Jefferson, St. John, St. Charles, St. James Ascension, Assumption, Terrebonne, Lafourche, St. Mary, St. Martin, and Orleans, including the City of New Orleans) MISSISSIPPI, ALABAMA, FLORIDA, GEORGIA, SOUTH CAROLINA, NORTH CAROLINA, and VIRGINIA, (except the forty-eight counties designated as West Virginia, and also the counties of Berkley, Accomac, Northampton, Elizabeth City, York, Princess Ann, and Norfolk, including the cities of Norfolk and Portsmouth), and which excepted parts, are for the present, left precisely as if this proclamation were not issued.

And by virtue of the power, and for the purpose aforesaid, I do order and declare that all persons held as slaves within said designated States, and parts of States, are, and henceforward shall be free; and that the Executive government of the United States, including the military and naval authorities thereof, will recognize and maintain the freedom of said persons.

And I hereby enjoin upon the people so declared to be free to abstain from all violence, unless in necessary self-defence; and I recommend to them that, in all cases when allowed, they labor faithfully for reasonable wages.

And I further declare and make known, that such persons of suitable condition, will be received into the armed service of the United States to garrison forts, positions, stations, and other places, and to man vessels of all sorts in said service.

And upon this act, sincerely believed to be an act of justice, warranted by the Constitution, upon military necessity, I invoke the considerate judgment of mankind, and the gracious favor of Almighty God.

In witness whereof, I have hereunto set my hand and caused the seal of the United States to be affixed.

Done at the CITY OF WASHINGTON, this first day of January, in the year of our Lord one thousand eight hundred and sixty three, and of the Independence of the United States of America the eighty-seventh.

By the President: *Abraham Lincoln*

William H. Seward, Secretary of State.

THE DISTRICT OF COLUMBIA EMANCIPATION ACT

President Abraham Lincoln signed the District of Columbia Emancipation Act on April 16, 1862, eight and a half months before he issued the Emancipation Proclamation. The act immediately freed all enslaved people within DC and paid former slaveholders up to $300 per freed person.

An Act

for the Release of certain Persons held to Service
or Labor in the District of Columbia

Be it enacted *by the Senate and House of Representatives of the United States of America in Congress assembled,* That all persons held to service or labor within the District of Columbia by reason of African descent are hereby discharged and freed of and from all claim to such service or labor; and from and after the passage of this act neither slavery nor involuntary servitude, except for crime, whereof the party shall be duly convicted, shall hereafter exist in said District.

Sec. 2. *And be it further enacted,* That all persons loyal to the United States, holding claims to service or labor against persons discharged therefrom by this act, may, within ninety days from the passage thereof, but not thereafter, present to the commissioners hereinafter mentioned their respective statements or petitions in writing, verified by oath or affirmation, setting forth the names, ages, and personal description of such persons, the manner in which said petitioners acquired such claim, and any facts touching the value thereof, and declaring his allegiance to the Government of the United States, and that he has not borne arms against the United States during the present rebellion, nor in any way given aid or comfort thereto: *Provided,* That the oath of the party to the petition shall not be evidence of the facts therein stated.

SEC. 3. *And be it further enacted*, That the President of the United States, with the advice and consent of the Senate, shall appoint three commissioners, residents of the District of Columbia, any two of whom shall have power to act, who shall receive the petitions above mentioned, and who shall investigate and determine the validity and value of the claims therein presented, as aforesaid, and appraise and apportion, under the proviso hereto annexed, the value in money of the several claims by them found to be valid: *Provided, however*, That the entire sum so appraised and apportioned shall not exceed in the aggregate an amount equal to three hundred dollars for each person shown to have been so held by lawful claim: *And provided, further*, That no claim shall be allowed for any slave or slaves brought into said District after the passage of this act, nor for any slave claimed by any person who has borne arms against the Government of the United States in the present rebellion, or in any way given aid or comfort thereto, or which originates in or by virtue of any transfer heretofore made, or which hereafter be made by any person who has in any manner aided or sustained the rebellion against the Government of the United States.

———

SEC. 4. *And be it further enacted*, That said commissioners shall, within nine months from the passage of this act, make a full and final report of their proceedings, findings, and appraisement, and shall deliver the same to the Secretary of the Treasury, which report shall be deemed and taken to be conclusive in all respects, except as hereinafter provided; and the

Secretary of the Treasury shall, with like exception, cause the amounts so apportioned to said claims to be paid from the Treasury of the United States to the parties found by said report to be entitled thereto as aforesaid, and the same shall be received in full and complete compensation: *Provided*, That in cases where petitions may be filed presenting conflicting claims, or setting up liens, said commissioners shall so specify in said report, and payment shall not be made according to the award of said commissioners until a period of sixty days shall have elapsed, during which time any petitioner claiming an interest in the particular amount may file a bill in equity in the Circuit Court of the District of Columbia, making all other claimants defendants thereto, setting forth the proceedings in such case before said commissioners and their actions therein, and praying that the party to whom payment has been awarded may be enjoined form receiving the same; and if said court shall grant such provisional order, a copy thereof may, on motion of said complainant, be served upon the Secretary of the Treasury, who shall thereupon cause the said amount of money to be paid into said court, subject to its orders and final decree, which payment shall be in full and complete compensation, as in other cases.

———

SEC. 5. *And be it further enacted,* That said commissioners shall hold their sessions in the city of Washington, at such place and times as the President of the United States may direct, of which they shall give due and public notice. They shall have power to subpoena and compel the attendance of witnesses, and to receive testimony and enforce its production, as in civil cases before courts of justice, without the exclusion of any witness on account of color; and they may summon before them the persons making claim to service or labor, and examine them under oath; and they may also, for purposes of identification and appraisement, call before them the persons so claimed. Said commissioners shall appoint a clerk, who shall keep files and complete record of all proceedings before them, who shall have power to administer oaths and affirmations in said proceedings, and who shall issue all lawful process by them ordered. The Marshal of the District of Columbia shall personally, or by deputy, attend upon the sessions of said commissioners, and shall execute the process issued by said clerk.

———

Sec. 6. *And be it further enacted*, That said commissioners shall receive in compensation for their services the sum of two thousand dollars each, to be paid upon the filing of their report; that said clerk shall receive for his services the sum of two hundred dollars per month; that said marshal shall receive such fees as are allowed by law for similar services performed by him in the Circuit Court of the District of Columbia; that the Secretary of the Treasury shall cause all other reasonable expenses of said commission to be audited and allowed, and that said compensation, fees, and expenses shall be paid from the Treasury of the United States.

———

Sec. 7. *And be it further enacted*, That for the purpose of carrying this act into effect there is hereby appropriated, out of any money in the Treasury not otherwise appropriated, a sum not exceeding one million of dollars.

———

SEC. 8. *And be it further enacted*, That any person or persons who shall kidnap, or in any manner transport or procure to be taken out of said District, any person or persons discharged and freed by the provisions of this act, or any free person or persons with intent to re-enslave or sell such person or person into slavery, or shall re-enslave any of said freed persons, the person of persons so offending shall be deemed guilty of a felony, and on conviction thereof in any court of competent jurisdiction in said District, shall be imprisoned in the penitentiary not less than five nor more that twenty years.

———

SEC. 9. *And be it further enacted*, That within twenty days, or within such further time as the commissioners herein provided for shall limit, after the passage of this act, a statement in writing or schedule shall be filed with the clerk of the Circuit court for the District of Columbia, by the several owners or claimants to the services of the persons made free or manumitted by this act, setting forth the names, ages, sex, and particular description of such persons, severally; and the said clerk shall receive and record, in a book by him to be provided and kept for that purpose, the said statements or schedules on receiving fifty cents each therefor, and no claim shall be allowed to any claimant or owner who shall neglect this requirement.

———

Sec. 10. *And be it further enacted*, That the said clerk and his successors in office shall, from time to time, on demand, and on receiving twenty-five cents therefor, prepare, sign, and deliver to each person made free or manumitted by this act, a certificate under the seal of said court, setting out the name, age, and description of such person, and stating that such person was duly manumitted and set free by this act.

———

Sec. 11. *And be it further enacted*, That the sum of one hundred thousand dollars, out of any money in the Treasury not otherwise appropriated, is hereby appropriated, to be expended under the direction of the President of the United States, to aid in the colonization and settlement of such free persons of African descent now residing in said District, including those to be liberated by this act, as may desire to emigrate to the Republics of Hayti or Liberia, or such other country beyond the limits of the United States as the President may determine: *Provided*, The expenditure for this purpose shall not exceed one hundred dollars for each emigrant.

———

Sec. 12. *And be it further enacted*, That all acts of Congress and all laws of the State of Maryland in force in said District, and all ordinances of the cities of Washington and Georgetown, inconsistent with the provisions of this act, are hereby repealed.

The abolition of slavery in the District of Columbia was one of the most important events connected with the prosecution of the war for the preservation of the Union, and, as such, is worthy of the marked commemoration we have given it to-day. It was not only a staggering blow to slavery throughout the country, but a killing blow to the rebellion, and was the beginning of the end to both.

—— FREDERICK DOUGLASS,
ADDRESS AT THE CONGREGATIONAL CHURCH,
WASHINGTON, DC, ON THE ANNIVERSARY
OF DC EMANCIPATION, APRIL 16, 1883

LAW ENACTING EMANCIPATION
IN THE
FEDERAL TERRITORIES

On June 19, 1862, Congress approved an act to "secure Freedom to all Persons within the Territories of the United States," which outlawed slavery in any current or future US territory. At the time, this included much of what is now the midwestern and western United States, such as the Colorado Territory, Dakota Territory, and Nevada Territory.

An Act

to secure Freedom to all Persons within the Territories
of the United States.

BE IT ENACTED *by the Senate and House of Representatives of the United States of America in Congress assembled,* That from and after the passage of this act there shall be neither slavery nor involuntary servitude in any of the Territories of the United States now existing, or which may at any time hereafter be formed or acquired by the United States, otherwise than in punishment of crimes whereof the party shall have been duly convicted.

APPROVED, June 19, 1862.

GENERAL ORDER
No. 3

Union general Gordon Granger issued General Order No. 3 on
June 19, 1865, informing the people of Texas of the Emancipation
Proclamation and its message that all enslaved people were free.
The day came to be known as Juneteenth and is now celebrated
as the end of slavery in the United States.

HEAD QUARTERS DISTRICT OF TEXAS
Galveston, Texas, June 19th, 1865.

General Orders, №. 3.

The people of Texas are informed that, in accordance with a proclamation from the Executive of the United States, all slaves are free. This involves an absolute equality of personal rights and rights of property between former masters and slaves, and the connection heretofore existing between them becomes that between employer and hired labor.

The freedmen are advised to remain quietly at their present homes and work for wages. They are informed that they will not be allowed to collect at military posts and that they will not be supported in idleness either there or elsewhere.

By order of   Major General GRANGER
                    F. W. EMERY, Major A. A. Genl.

THIRTEENTH, FOURTEENTH, AND FIFTEENTH AMENDMENTS

The Thirteenth, Fourteenth, and Fifteenth Amendments formally abolished slavery in the United States, gave all citizens equal protection under the law, and prohibited discrimination in the voting rights of citizens based on race, color, or previous enslavement. These amendments, ratified between 1865 and 1870, are known as the Reconstruction Amendments.

Amendment XIII
Passed by Congress January 31, 1865
Ratified December 6, 1865

Neither slavery nor involuntary servitude, except as a punishment for crime whereof the party shall have been duly convicted, shall exist within the United States, or any place subject to their jurisdiction.

SECTION 2. Congress shall have power to enforce this article by appropriate legislation.

Amendment XIV
Passed by Congress June 13, 1866
Ratified July 9, 1868

All persons born or naturalized in the United States, and subject to the jurisdiction thereof, are citizens of the United States and of the State wherein they reside. No State shall make or enforce any law which shall abridge the privileges or immunities of citizens of the United States; nor shall any State deprive any person of life, liberty, or property, without due process of law; nor deny to any person within its jurisdiction the equal protection of the laws.

SECTION 2. Representatives shall be apportioned among the several States according to their respective numbers, counting the whole number of persons in each State, excluding Indians not taxed. But when the right to vote at any election for the choice of electors for President and Vice-President of the United States,

Representatives in Congress, the Executive and Judicial officers of a State, or the members of the Legislature thereof, is denied to any of the male inhabitants of such State, being twenty-one years of age, and citizens of the United States, or in any way abridged, except for participation in rebellion, or other crime, the basis of representation therein shall be reduced in the proportion which the number of such male citizens shall bear to the whole number of male citizens twenty-one years of age in such State.

———

SECTION 3. No person shall be a Senator or Representative in Congress, or elector of President and Vice-President, or hold any office, civil or military, under the United States, or under any State, who, having previously taken an oath, as a member of Congress, or as an officer of the United States, or as a member of any State legislature, or as an executive or judicial officer of any State, to support the Constitution of the United States, shall have engaged in insurrection or rebellion against the same, or given aid or comfort to the enemies thereof. But Congress may by a vote of two-thirds of each House, remove such disability.

———

SECTION 4. The validity of the public debt of the United States, authorized by law, including debts incurred for payment of pensions and bounties for services in suppressing insurrection or rebellion, shall not be questioned. But neither the United States nor any State shall assume or pay any debt or obligation incurred in aid of insurrection or rebellion against the United States, or any claim for the loss or emancipation of any slave; but all such debts, obligations and claims shall be held illegal and void.

———

SECTION 5. The Congress shall have the power to enforce, by appropriate legislation, the provisions of this article.

Amendment XV
Passed by Congress February 26, 1869
Ratified February 3, 1870.

———

SECTION 1. The right of citizens of the United States to vote shall not be denied or abridged by the United States or by any State on account of race, color, or previous condition of servitude—

———

SECTION 2. The Congress shall have the power to enforce this article by appropriate legislation.

THE
PROCLAMATION
OF
EMANCIPATION;
BY THE
PRESIDENT
OF THE
UNITED STATES,
TO TAKE EFFECT
JANUARY 1st, 1863.